GW00585395

SPACE

First published in 2022 by
The Dedalus Press
13 Moyclare Road
Baldoyle
Dublin D13 K1C2
Ireland

www.dedaluspress.com

ISBN 978-1-910251-98-0 (paperback)
ISBN 978-1-910251-99-7 (hardback)

Dedalus Press titles are available in Ireland
from Argosy Books (www.argosybooks.ie) and in the UK
from Inpress Books (www.inpressbooks.co.uk).

Printed in Ireland by Print Dynamics, Dublin.

Cover image: *Confluence of Thinking* by Diana Copperwhite,
oil on canvas, 120 x 120 cm, 2021.
www.dianacopperwhite.net

The Dedalus Press receives financial assistance from
The Arts Council / An Chomhairle Ealaíon.

SPACE

JOHN KELLY

DEDALUS PRESS

ACKNOWLEDGEMENTS

My thanks to Diana Copperwhite for kind permission to use her painting *Confluence of Thinking* on the cover.

A number of these poems have appeared in various literary journals and anthologies. I'm grateful to the editors of *The Stinging Fly*, *Poetry Ireland Review*, *Moth*, *Banshee*, *Manchester Review*, *The Irish Review* and *Oxford Magazine*. 'Synecdoche and Metonym' and '1981' first appeared in *Port*, Issue 25, ed. Dan Crowe, guest ed. Cillian Murphy. 'Walking the Dog' first appeared in *Local Wonders: Poems of our Immediate Surrounds*, Dedalus Press, 2021, ed. Pat Boran. 'I Was Full of Wine When the Call Came' was read at *Miscellany 50: Live at the Project* and later appeared in *Miscellany 50: Fifty Years of Sunday Miscellany*, ed. Clíodhna Ní Anluain. 'The Ray-Gun,' 'Lapwings in Cavan' and 'The Long Game' first appeared in *The New Frontier: Reflections from the Irish Border*, ed. James Conor Patterson.

The lines from Dante's *Inferno*, which form the epigraph to 'Booterstown', are from *The Divine Comedy*, translated by C.H. Sisson (Oxford World's Classics).

My deepest gratitude to my editor Pat Boran for his support, care and attention in the making of this book.

Contents

⁓

for Catherine

The Ray-Gun

It was plastic with a perfect moulded grip;
silver with a see-through cylinder
and a cosmos of coloured cogs that turned
when you squeezed the trigger.

The best part was the sparks that flew
in the black hole of the coal-shed –
a stone-age mystery involving flint
that also lit the barrel up in sci-fi red.

The trigger, come to think of it,
was crooked, unreliable and made of tin –
when it nipped your finger, the blood
would float, in blobs, from your spaceman skin.

Older weapons couldn't go outside at all –
my Colt revolvers holstered and forbidden –
but something silvery and space-age
would surely never be mistaken

by an unmarked car or itchy foot patrol.
Not that my constant pal was much concerned –
an *army-man* with Tommy gun and camouflage
he was on always on parade. Saluting. Presenting arms.

One time on the Cam River, we saw a mink.
Boot-black, it bounced through the grass
as my pal took deadly aim. *The law's the law,* he said,
and, eagerly, he swore he'd tell the police.

But I said a prayer to a black Peruvian saint
that the bright-eyed mink would get away.
Then the trigger and the sparks
and the sudden shadow of a Martian craft.

The Hereafter

Nobody knows it's here.
You can't see it from the road
or the mountain, or the bog.
It's so well hidden it's a mystery
even to the lake to which it flows.

Usually, it's barely here at all –
just a trickle over whitened stones –
but when cold rain falls
for days on end, the secret river
fills and runs and swells.

Everything's perfected then
in a cool, fluorescent atmosphere –
sunlit black and lime-green banks,
jewelled gravel set for trout.
Enter here by rowboat. Disappear.

A Different Time

When I was a child
I would catch wild hares

with my two bare hands.
Their eyesight is so bad

that, if the wind was right,
you could sneak up close enough

to dive like Tarzan on the biggest one,
then grab and hold it to your chest.

I loved to feel their fur,
their knobbly, velvety bones.

Nobody would believe you
if you said that now. But it's true.

I sat so still one time
that a hare just hobbled up to me

and stepped across my shoes.
But then nobody believes we had kingfishers

either. Or, for that matter,
bats and poltergeists.

Derrychara

When nougat was *nugget*
and Renault was Ren*awlt*

and Ajax of Amsterdam
was said the same way

as Ajax, the all-purpose cleaner
or the fearless hero of Troy –

he who led the Greek attacks
and covered all retreats;

when Gerd 'Der Bomber' Müller
hadn't an umlaut to his name

and Madrid was not Real but *real*
and I got stuck on *delicatessen*

while reading Minnie the Minx
because we'd no such thing in Enniskillen,

I could have told you, all the same,
what brand of religion you were

by how you said aloud
the townland name of Derrychara –

with the hard *ch* of church
or aspirated and without.

Derry*ch*ara or *Derraharra* –
that's to say Doire Chara

meaning the oakwood of the weir.
Or, as a friend of mine suggested,

Doire *Chora* meaning pot,
cauldron or swirling pool.

Orchard Street

On Orchard Street on Sunday
she saw her handsome, murdered twin.

He was frisking all the jackets
that hung high like suicides

or swung on sidewalk rails
like rows of executed men.

When finally he'd vanished
in the throng, she searched herself

for sense and knew it wasn't him.
It was just some guy

from Westchester or Riverdale
back in the old neighbourhood

looking for a bargain, or at least
the rumoured memory of same.

Autograph

In the afterlight of a circus tent,
his close-up face deranged with paint,
he stood alone and smoked –
parallels at half-mast, patchwork blouse,
squirting flower, giant bedpan shoes.

And as he signed his name for me –
this famous clown – the circus mistress
swooped and grabbed my wrist and ripped
and threw my small memento to the ground –
the pencil-scribbled syllables of silly baby sounds.

I never mentioned it again.
That woman's cruel beak, her vicious witch's eyes
and how, ferociously, she ordered both of us away –
me to my pebbledashed estate; him to lion-stink
and a slapstick mess of broken plates.

So I learned that clowns are all pretend
and villains, funny enough, are not.
I'll not forget the hilt of her stupid whip,
the underarm rip in her angry, hunting coat.
The clownish name I cannot yet write out.

Origin Myth

And the whole earth was of one language, and of one speech.
—*Genesis 11:1*

There was a colour plate in the Bible –
The (Great) Tower of Babel

painted by the elder Pieter Bruegel,
and if you put your ear to the page

you'd hear a mad clatter of languages –
Fingallian, Cam, Forth and Bargy –

that's to say, Yola – and a whole handlin'
of Middle, Modern and my own Hibernobéarla.

But it's only now I'm wondering
why, above the *ruaille buaille* of that addled, orgiastic din –

Anglo-Norman, Greek and Vulgar Latin –
was there no *anseo, ansiúd* or *ansin*?

By which I mean *within* the tower itself;
inside that quare and God-offending ziggurat.

The Western Education and Library Board

When I asked the old librarian
for a book about Concorde –
all the rage (if not the talk of the town)
in those supersonic days,

she looked me up and down
and quoted me *verbatim* to a man
reading *Boys and Girls of the British World*
by a creaking Superser.

Indeed we do not, she said at last,
like she was licking packet soup
from the carcass of a cat, we don't
stock filthy books the like of that!

To be fair, perhaps she'd never heard of Concorde
and never hoped to see its nose poking from a hangar
at Heathrow, or hear its mighty sonic boom in the skies
above *Par-ee,* but sometimes it occurs to me

that if not for this bitter, dark *débâcle*
I might have been (if not a pilot and a playboy)
a falconer at Charles de Gaulle, a raptor on my fist;
my only job in life to keep the local pests away.

The St. Michael's Day Massacre

for Séamas MacAnnaidh

There were force fields in our school –
bold white lines shot across the tarmac
disintegrating those who dared to cross,
leaving little piles of schoolboy ash
to be scattered on the roses late at night.

They switched them off in case
of accidents the day the bishop came –
the day my year was blown to bits.
Not zapped but riddled – filled full of lead
by the old-school Father Monaghan,
kneeling devoutly behind his car
with a fag and a naggin and a Gatling gun.

Hugh Keenan

On the 9th February 1909
God Save the King
was played seventeen times
by a dutiful German band.

And all on the platform
of Brandenburg station,
and everyone waiting
for Saxe-Coburg and Gotha

to get his uniform on –
his *Zeremonienschwert*
in his wandering
königliche hand.

Five years later Hugh Keenan,
with no great *grá*
(as far as I'm aware)
for neither King nor Kaiser –

by this stage George V,
the newly-minted Windsor,
and his ridiculous cousin Bill –
put on the woollen uniform

of (I think) the Inniskilling Fusiliers
and went away to war –
khaki Pattern Service Dress,
puttees, forage cap and haversack.

In any event, he lived, returned,
and never told the tale.
Not a single word of slaughter,
medals, flags or swords –

just that single mention once
of dogfights over France,
and how he'd raised his eyes
from a rat-filled trench and saw

the blood-red Fokker triplane
of Manfred Albrecht Freiherr von Richthofen –
The Red Baron himself.
Out of the sun. Looping the loop.

1981

It was the end of May –
posters were up and black flags flew
and, beyond the bridge, swallows
in countless numbers, looped
their scribbled patterns on the Erne.

Summer's possibility had begun
but I was still at school, enduring
the last few weeks of term
when the hours thickened, and the clock
stuttered back and forth to half past three

and all I wanted to be was out in a boat –
off to the islands where the skeleton bones
of mammals and birds lay where they'd fallen
in the unmowed grass. Islands with cuckoos
and Sheela na Gigs, and pathways made by hares.

If, on the way back, a chopper – a Lynx or a Gazelle –
zoomed across and buzzed the boat, and a soldier
from Blaydon-on-Tyne lined you up in his rifle's sight,
what else could you do but hold your course?
Go home. Do your homework. Watch the news.

Maguire Compares Himself to Jesus

The Heavens open at Devenish,
but he strips regardless
and steps with purpose through the reeds,
white shins stampeding the waterhens,
white thighs scattering the fry.

He jokes about the Jordan –
making more of his dip
than is decent and wise,
but he is thirty now, just turned,
and the Lough, for once, is warm.

To go under is the vital thing –
down like a cormorant, up like a salmon
to thrash and kick in limestone whirls.
And then, not like himself at all,
to scream and whoop and roar.

After that – a stick-man afloat on his back –
he waits, almost prayerfully, for the clouds
to part and The Holy Ghost to plummet –
tail-feathers fanned. Drumming.
Nearly like a snipe.

Home

Like a wary traveller at the door,
she'd ask me first about the corncrake
and if I ever heard its call.

It was, I used to think, a simple question –
nothing cosmic, deep or existential –
she was, I just assumed, adjusting to a time

to which she had returned.
To tell the truth, she might as well
have asked if Victoria was on her throne,

if Hitler was the Chancellor, or if the border
at Blacklion was now some kind of fact.
It's a wonder that she never asked

if we were, the two of us, by any chance related.
Was I perhaps her father, or her brother
or her son? And did Mulherns still have the pub?

This summer's day, with a son of my own,
I'm asking if he's seen or heard the swifts,
for I've spotted only four this year

and I remember when they used to screech in dozens,
hurled in squadrons by the Gods themselves
as, mesmerized, I stood on Darling Street, surrounded.

But when was that? And who was I?
And was I myself at all, stock still
in The Brook, Hall's Lane or Paget Square?

It must have been before
they tossed the backs of things – the beautiful,
imperfect bricks of workshops and stables,

blacksmiths, bellhangers and people's homes;
all those tiny gaps in townie buildings
where the swift-admitting slates had slipped a little.

Barking

It's not that I don't know where I am, exactly,
but sometimes, when I waken from a dream,
I can never conjure up the outside world at all;

can bring to mind neither front nor back;
can picture neither street nor quiet garden
emptied of its foxes now but filled with songster birds.

Sometimes what comes first
are the sunlit curtains of my childhood room,
then the Arctic air of our old estate,

then the shrieks of unleashed kids
making slides, throwing snowballs,
rolling snowmen torsos up and down the hill.

Perhaps the cause of it is this: some nights I fall asleep
to barking dogs – some as far away as Wicklow –
voices I know from fifty-something years ago –

patterns, pitch and rhythms I seem to recognise.
The decent, long-dead dogs of Enniskillen.
Caesar Curry, Paddy Dooris, Bonzo Hynes.

Woodwork

for Eric Mingus

1

I would not have been contemplating
the resemblance between motion and stasis

had I not been wide awake, reading
Brodsky's *Daedalus In Sicily*

and wondering how, as a younger man,
long before the heifer and the labyrinth,

or the wings on which he ultimately fled,
the father of carpentry had already

invented, perhaps for his son,
a joyous machine called a seesaw.

A collaboration of equals.
To do with the physics of lever and torque.

2

My father loved the story of Icarus.
He'd tell it with a sketchpad on his knee
so he could draw for me, with a 2B pencil, the falling boy.

I can't recall if Daedalus himself was ever drawn
or even mentioned by his name – he was just the father
who had made the wings and made it clear:

too close to the sun and the wax will melt,
too close to the sea and the feathers will soak.

I wonder if my father, a carpenter by trade,
already knew that Daedalus invented carpentry?
Did it ever cross his mind as he turned the page,

pared another pencil and drew so perfectly,
with a carpenter's hand, the primary feathers
of various birds in a suddenly empty sky.

3

I remember, after work,
how he'd sit on the settee
and lay his hand palm-upwards
on my mother's knee.

She'd lift his fingers gently
and, with a needle from the tin,
remove a splinter
from the soft parts of his skin.

Quietly, he'd watch the news
but I'd see him bite his lip
as she worked some skelf of spruce
gone in awkwardly and deep.

In recent times, cold sober
and dead to TV's dark alarms,
I also bite my lip and wonder
would it do more harm

than good to painstakingly
remove whatever's jagging
lately in my brain. Or name
the things that run in families

like tiny, festering chips
of cedar, pine or oak.
Put a good leadwood in water,
he told me once, and it will sink.

4

And yes, I did get the present
a little Jesus would have asked for –
a carpentry set
with a mallet, a hammer, a chisel
and a saw that wouldn't cut butter.

I wondered if Jesus ever
wanted to raid his father's bag
to handle a real saw – one with crooked teeth –
one to eat through crosses
or the boards of next door's fence.

My father's bag with loose nails,
sawdust, awls and bits,
real deadly chisels, a plane that would skin you
and a claw hammer to bury six-inch nails
and pull them out again.

5.

In the days before Christmas,
at the civil, well-planed bar
of Dublin's Long Hall pub,
I sat with my buddy Eric
(among other things a carpenter)
talking quietly about the Mob –
in the movies and for real –
and a brush with John Gotti
that night in New York. But mostly
we talked joinery and jazz
as, solemnly, we toasted our dads.

Who first mentioned Jesus
is not too clear. These days
Jesus rarely features, even at Christmas,
but it was Eric, for sure, who said
that, as per certain lost accounts, Joseph,
while no doubt the model father,
as a carpenter was no great shakes –
forgotten kerfs and such, and nothing ever square.
His M.O. though, for every shoddy build
was to get the lad to do his tricks
and *zap!* The wonky table's fixed!

Joseph, barely mentioned in Bible,
is almost always old – a balding bystander
in holy pictures and rarely on his own.
I marvelled at the one by de La Tour –
a working man, his sleeves rolled,
and light shining through the young boy's hand.
The best ones, though, are by Thomas Kelly and Giotto –
the latter in Padua, the former in the parlour
of the Convent of Mercy in Enniskillen –
painted when two nuns arrived at the house
and made my father an offer he couldn't refuse.

6.

And then there was that other Joseph –
of Cupertino aka The Flying Friar –

Franciscan ecstatic and carpenter's son
who, if he thought of anything at all,

might well have considered his father
as he flew around the church

helping workmen high up in the roof beams,
zooming up and down, carrying their materials,

retrieving any mallets, callipers, chisels or planes
that had dropped like unexpected music to the floor.

And under his own steam too!
No need for wings or complex apparatus.

The Patron Saint of Aviators, they say he flew
a hundred times and hovered high above the trees,

and sometimes swooped, a tad recklessly, through the refectory
flourishing a sea urchin like a red-hot Sacred Heart.

7.

The shed needs repairs
well beyond my capabilities –
the porch part in particular –
banjaxed like the broken shacks
I passed on hidden tributaries
of the Tallapoosa and the Mississippi –
the KEEP OUT signs, the beaten dogs,
the Confederate, fully-loaded flags.

But I love my shed and rush to it
in downpours just to listen to the rain
then, at the open door, inhale the petrichor.
My father's tools are stored here now –
some bought with his first apprentice wage.
With this hacksaw, rule and mortise gauge
I could make myself a holy picture. The arch
of the porch like the middle panel of a triptych.

The Beech

The beech is bare. Here where
I still intend, when this is over,
to build a hut – a place to sit,
to think quietly and straight
and, with pleasure, isolate.

It's the end of March
and ever since September
I've inspected the mast –
these brown shining nips of nut
that feed the squirrels in the frost.

The dried-up, muddied shells
are scattered now like helmets after Troy,
or that plague of snails we saw in Italy
flow like lava through the woods,
down the hill, across the crunching road.

Today, as I pace the warming flags
in scuffed and unlaced boots,
the beechnut shells are crushed
like all the limpets and the razor shells
piled up on the beach beyond –

the strand where I might see,
if I climbed the rigging of this tree,
a lanky figure on the move, his two eyes shut,
and a schooner on the slowing sea – dark and silent,
almost absent, triple-masted.

Barrelman. Mad bastard on the *qui vive*
I could perch up there for weeks,
up where the magpies build their nest,
where the branches bear my weight
and leaves will soon erase my silhouette.

Lapwings in Cavan

for Lisa O'Neill

I miss that swerve of road
where lapwings used to muster in the field.
I'd see them and be settled and relieved

and think out loud (Old English)
hleapewince, phillipene,
plover, peewit, pilibín.

Leaper-winker maybe so,
but if ever wings deserved a word like *lap* –
in fact, the only word for it is *flap*

when, haphazardly, they slap the skies
like flying cloths, and even more so
now they're getting scarce.

I wonder what the landmark is
for them – the birds' eye view –
when what they see is always something new.

Is it the bypass or the roundabout?
The Applegreen – the forecourt and the lights?
Or just the other pilibíns tumbling in fits and starts?

Somewhere in Pascal's *Pensées*
it says, *How many kingdoms know nothing of us!*
This dwindling kingdom of birds perhaps –

Vanellus vanellus, winnowing fans;
nesting, feeding; flickering above and to the side
of our new and smooth and unobstructed road.

The Toad

The toad made for the pool.
Lumpily, it struggled
like a walking footstool

or the squattest Ottoman.
A coal-man with a leather cowl –
silent, joyless, burdened down.

The black, carbuncled carapace.
The pressured, anxious,
weighted gaze

beneath the hoisted bag of slack.
Andalucía. Anthracite.
A cruel memory of piggy-back.

Dead Tree with Six Vultures

You'd nearly think the scene
was pre-arranged – a tableau

somehow set for only us to see:
a volt of Old World vultures –

white-backed, Old Testament
and bent like battered angels.

Not cherubim or seraphim
but angels all the same –

prodigious wings by Botticelli,
Fra Angelico, Van Eyck

but with that added, heightened whiff
of carnage, blood and rot.

Is this the tree from Genesis?
Can this be Eden emptied out?

Mackerel

There was mortal shock in that swallowed *thup* –
the deep and instant plumb drop
as hooks and feathers plummeted
like a host of fallen angels into slate.

The whole thing seemed unstoppable,
like the paying out of graveside rope,
until some deep and unseen frenzy
shook the rod and sent you

skywards to grip and lift and reel.
And then you saw them! Mackerel!
Like a chandelier lit with death.
A frantic mirror ball of fear.

Hoist, and most would slap and shudder at your feet,
the foul-hooked ones you dared not think about.
But that night, when each was cleaned and cooked
and eaten up with salt and lemon juice,

you'd fall asleep to liftings and to lowerings,
to sun and splash and sparkling saltiness.
You'd dream the very boat, the ocean's rise and fall.
The downward baited line. The upward glitter-haul.

Woodcock

A pair – male and female – in a wintry display
of cinnamon twigs, ferns and sugar-dusted leaves.
A Midwinter idyll, almost as if they'd never

been flushed and shot and mounted;
now ignored in a corridor of abandoned books
and Edwardian steamer trunks.

Cryptic, elusive, under-recorded,
there's a touch of alien craft about the woodcock –
the helmeted head, the set of the eyes,

the bill a transmitter and probe. Gyroscopes
in the skull for multidirectional flight
on their long cold journeys to the moon.

Tonight the moon is full. You retire early
and I take my second night-cap to the door
to quietly consider Derryclare, Benbaun, Bencorr.

Imagine all the dogs and men who hunted here.
All dead – the taxidermist too – and so we'll never know
if the woodcock in corridor were separately shot

or were ever, truly, together in life – his lightness
on her lightness in the dark of the rhododendrons,
or the moonlight of the middle slopes.

Back upstairs neither one of them has moved. No closer
and no further apart, but set for space flight all the same.
Two woodcock, posing, in a kind of fish-tank. Game.

I Was Full of Wine When the Call Came

I was full of wine when the call came.
Our kids and the neighbours' kids
were all done-up like zombies –
stitched-up corpses with white faces,
black eyeliner and fake blood.
On the floor, a red plastic basin
swayed like small, woozy sea –
bits of floating apple already turning brown,
dishcloths soaking up the spill.
No need to ruin it, I thought.
Tomorrow would be time enough.
I put a black tie in my pocket and I left.

Halloween. A night I used to love.
Sweaty false-faces from Wellworths,
Fanta, fruit and monkey nuts.
And, though I couldn't name it then,
that thrilling rip in everything as spirits,
manes and shades walked abroad on our estates.
I wore a vampire's cloak my mother made
from the blackout curtain that saved Eden Street
from the Luftwaffe in 1941.
The undead cast no shadow, or so they said,
but mine was on the footpath, arms spread wide.
And I loved the flowing, phantom shape of me in flight.

So, as Halloween slipped into All-Saints,
and my mother slipped closer to her death,
I, not fit to drive, was on the last bus north,
forced by its own sobering schedule
onto old forgotten roads, turning hard
into bypassed places like Navan and Cavan and Kells.

That slow crow over Dalkey, I kept thinking,
and a week of not sleeping and bad dreams.
And all the time my mother, who never drank or smoked,
was feeling no pain in the South West Acute.
Adrenalin too, they told me later,
keeping her on earth until I got there.

The driver was a speed merchant.
Like a man who'd left the immersion on
he blarged on through the black beyond Belturbet
and up and over the vanished border.
I imagined a mountain pass in Transylvania
and him lashing at his horses in a thunderstorm,
our *calèche* hurtling to the land beyond the forest.
Or else a long-haul flight at night in heavy turbulence,
when you check the screen to see where you are,
and you're somewhere over Syria or Iraq
and up ahead, it's Mosul and Baghdad.
Nothing but mad drivers, she'd have said.

They say that hearing is the last to go,
so she'd have heard the slowing, vital beeps,
my questions and the nurses' sympathetic chat –
all that talk of screens and dropping numbers
as the body persevered.
A heart like a lion, the nurse behind me said,
but, in the end, my mother held my hands
as if to teach the toddler me to walk,
or perhaps to join her in a dance.
And in the middle of all the mystery
and the no-great-mystery of death,
I was still afraid she'd smell the Merlot on my breath.

Devotions

The cold clarity of October nights –
windows lit on the dark road home,
the air full of coal-dust, stars and slack.

I miss all that. The chill, the prayers,
the cosy certainty that pyjamas
are waiting, warming in the press.

House of Gold.
Ark of the Covenant.
Gate of Heaven. Morning Star.

I knew these terms from early on;
words like *sacrament* and *reverence;*
the difference between a venal and a mortal sin.

But perhaps what's served me better since
was when, on frosty nights, putting out the bins,
I'd hear, then see, the whooper swans

whoosh low above the glittering slates.
Or wrapped up my duffle coat,
I'd be staring at the Pleiades;

swinging carelessly, contentedly,
on the creaking hinges of the gate,
and suddenly, again, that ghostly

whomping flight. Tonight, expecting them to pass,
I see them swooping down the Milky Way,
the Northern Cross – the brightest lights of Cygnus.

Spiritual Vessel,
Vessel of Honour, Singular Vessel
of Devotion, Mystical Rose.

Even now I can't make head nor tail
of this or any galaxy. Cosmology
and dark matter; stars, gas and dust.

Mother of Christ, Star of the Sea.
The swans, the gate, the Pleiades.
Pray for the wanderer, pray for me.

Booterstown

"And so they went away on the dark water;
And even before they had been disembarked,
Another flock had collected on this side."
—Dante. Inferno III.118–120

Darkness. Misted. Gurgling on its glacial till,
the hidden Trimleston, the Nutley stream
that gently brings the salt sea in.

Herons – Charons – hunched
in thick salinity: the very thing
that rarefies the place for plants and birds.

Egret, godwit, knot,
shelduck, dunlin, snipe.
Horsetail, bistort, creeping bent

and, rarest plant of all,
Borrer's Saltmarsh-grass.
Threatened species: vulnerable.

So when, again, my train expires,
the carriage lit for winter rain
here where stream and sea conspire,

I curse and press my forehead
to the dirty, steamed-up glass –
caught, once more, between the quick and the dead;

between the thriving and the almost extinct.

A Dream of Wexford in the Indian Ocean

First a zebra dove and me –
sheltering on the balcony
from a grey tropical downpour
that will never, ever stop.

I'm on two chairs turned
to face each other, jammed in tight
the way they'd make a cot for me
when I was small enough to fit,

and the bird is ragged with rain.
The banyan trees are blurring, machine-gun
downpour sparking off the leaves;
the ocean view is wiped away and gone.

When, days later, the sky clears up
and everything glows once more
with turquoise, gold and green –
the muddy pasture, palm and tractor tyres –

two woodpeckers are working on an oak.
In my sleep I have followed the sound
and found them easily enough – black and white
and red – the same pair that bred in Wexford.

They see me too. They stop.
Then, side by side, manoeuvring strangely,
more like butterflies than birds,
they fly towards me where I lie,

embracing mid-air, melding to a bright
and shiny ball that hits me right between the eyes.
The zebra dove is calling still – *croo-croo-croo* –
the alarm clock on the morning of our honeymoon.

Country House Hotel

The mist was unexpected –
the dark wash of woodland
as I stepped out on the lawn.

Jackdaws warmed themselves
on chimney pots.
The boom of a distant dog.

And as you slept on
in your too-soft bed,
dreaming and un-kissed,

I found for you
the snowflake of a barn owl
that was only said to exist.

Scops

I loved to shelter by the road
and scope the trees for all the sounds I heard.

This when rain would tick the leaves, and tap
on sheets of corrugated iron in the grass.

Even better were the first erotic drops of storm –
the drum, the sonic shapes that form

on *umberellas* (if you had the lend)
or the tightened flysheet of a tent.

All this week, dry as a stick, in a deep Greek valley,
a single owl ignites the dark machinery

of night. A lonesome sonar echoes up the slope –
the one sad note along our treacherous, blacked-out road.

But when answered back and all the notes begin to phase,
the pleasure, like the dark, is fathomless.

Anaïs

+31 6 479 79
879

anaisposkoviccull@gmail.com

The Long Game

We met them in the bush –
painted dogs in all directions –
and, sightings-wise, a real result.
They'd chased a leopard up a tree
and robbed its disembowelled kill,

but all I could see was Ballinaquill's U12s
loosed from their green, enamelled bus,
spilling onto our imperfect grass
in their violent, bony arrogance.
A crooked border parish famous for it still.

Their arrival was obscene – a yelping chaos
of swerving shoulders and lunging limbs;
the ugly, trotting menace of the one in front –
his too-long neck, his too-large head swaying blindly,
dead eyes rolling for our blood.

Today, our leopard waited in his tree.
Outnumbered, he'd forgo though not forget
the painted dogs' immeasurable offence.
He'd get them all again – that ringleader for sure –
when, that is, he'd spot the perfect chance.

Maybe next year at the big boys' school,
or on some future blacked-out street.
Or one day, in a poem at dawn,
whispered in the long grass, over coffee,
near the border with Mozambique.

Space

When Mrs Adams tapped the blackboard
with a red fingernail and spoke of *space*

and why I must put *space* between my words,
all I could see were the planets and the stars –

Saturn's rings, crescent moons, the Milky Way,
Cassiopeia scratched and scraping up and down.

Cosmonauts floated like giant babies
between words like *Mum* and *Dad,*

Laika the mongrel yelped at the universe
between *dog* and *cat,* and elsewhere

in the dusty nebulae of green and yellow chalk,
three American spacemen said their prayers,

pressed all the buttons in Apollo 13
and thought, tearfully, of home.

This morning as all the little stars,
newly formed in constellations,

lined out in Cabinteely Park
for their first competitive match,

I watched my son in his outsized jersey
chase a huge moon of a ball, and try

to make sense of yet more adult instruction –
the Mums and the Dads, the dog on the pitch,

the coach shouting, *Space! Space!*
Take your time, buddy! You have space!

Pilgrim in the Dark

From Phoenix
to Monument Valley
is a deep five-hour dream –

300 miles of Emmylou and Gram
through blacked-out panoramas
and nothing as it seems.

I've been round these parts before –
Flagstaff, Tuba City, the Hopi Reservation,
the parched, peered-into seabed of the Navajo Nation,

I know this cool eternity, black as death –
the buttes and mesas that I sense but cannot see.
State-line. Star-blanket. Appaloosas loose on US-163.

The car rolls on through midnight –
the utter darkness, the desert's outer space,
and then the gratitude at dawn

when I waken up, still breathing.
Mind-blown. No notion how I got here,
and for the second time.

Contentment Comes

not when tyres beat a metre
on lumpy slabs of American road

but on our own smooth motorway;
no traffic, driving south.

You're listening to music –
Mothership Connection on repeat –

and just as shutter speeds
can sometimes match the beat

of a flower-sucker's wings,
the wipers, just before they slip,

are, for a mile or so,
perfectly in sync.

The empty road swoops home
and, for a time, contentment comes,

the beat of wipers
exactly on the one.

Mythology

High in the mountains of somewhere,
in a language I can never remember,
there was a barmaid who chatted like a chiffchaff
and, later, as the night grew thicker, a wren.

Her lover in the corner, slim like a pearl diver,
was ponytailed and tanned. He sat before
a pint of local gin and never stirred,
just stared with tender focus at his glass.

In the nearest tarnished mirror
I listened to her talk of weather
and the several meanings of death,
and I swear she never took a breath

until the cocks began to crow
and I paid her with a ball of notes that showed
armoured kings leaning drunkenly on swords,
and ancient writers in their robes.

In the heat and rot of her father's barn
she carved a rusted serpent on my arm.
Wolves trotted by. Ravens clattered the skies.
The Gods, she kept repeating, *will punish us all.*

Synecdoche or Metonym

For a week I gazed at Ithaca –
mythic and wasp-waisted island
across a glittering three-mile strait.

And one day, as light clouds drifted
and the pareidolia took hold,
I saw the wise Penelope on plumped-up

pillows, and long-suffering Odysseus,
full-bearded, strapped to a ship
that quickly faded to a wisp.

Coffee grounds smoked in the ashtray.
I drank cheap Cephallenian white,
and, even though libations had been made,

when the shadows of two paragliders
darkened the day and cooled my skin
I knew the Gods were moving in.

Was it Zeus, the Cloud-gatherer?
Or worse, the Earthshaker?
I feared the latter and, sure enough,

the next morning at seven,
in what I took to be a bomb,
Lord Poseidon shook me wide-awake.

My very first earthquake
and, much like a bomb,
it's impossible to properly recall –

the boom, the blast, the shudder,
the falling masonry, the after-silence
and dark speculation of it all.

Years ago, I tried to write
about our most notorious one –
I was lying in my bed that morning too.

The sound of coffins falling,
tumbling at the gable wall. But no.
A bomb's a noise remembered only

when another one goes off –
or a ruined house collapses down a hill
into an olive grove.

Is it *synecdoche* or *metonym*
when Enniskillen – as in *another Enniskillen* –
means a bomb with very many dead?

Outside, the wasps were mad with figs,
cats asked questions in the shade,
swallows swooped to kiss the turquoise pool.

Corfu

for Theo Dorgan

There's a rock in the bay
called the Ship of Odysseus.

It proves, the scholars say,
that this was once Phaeacia –

home to those who rowed the hero back to Ithaca
after all that he'd been through.

Of course, I never knew,
as our ferry docked there until Dawn,

that on the very beach where I would sleep,
the locals saw that swift-returning ship

transformed incredibly to stone
by an unrelenting god;

or that beneath my aching shoulder blades
on the cool, uneven sand

they'd killed a dozen bulls in sacrifice,
burned bones and tasted inward meats,

all in case Poseidon, in endless rage,
would, with mountain ranges, hem their city in.

But I know it now and am confounded,
recalling stars, and dogs that sniffed my neck.

I see a black ship at anchor in the dark
and the goddess who had sunbathed on the deck.

In the end, perhaps no journey's ever wasted.
Even the ones you never knew you'd taken.

Dogma

In the dry hills above Malaga
there's a goldfinch held captive
in a shop that sells ice-cream to tourists.

I would toss that place, and I should,
but I've protested things before
only to find no other pilgrim shares my rage.

Or worse again, only for the goldfinch itself,
or the bullfinch or the siskin
to hop, still singing, back into the cage.

Jerusalem Syndrome

*Jerusalem Syndrome refers to a set of mental disorders triggered by
a visit to Jerusalem. In some cases it can involve delusional or psychotic
experiences where the sufferer believes that he or she is a character
from the Bible.*

Work took me to Jerusalem
and one night, as the crew slept,
myself and Art Ó Briain went for a jar
on Ben Yehuda Street.

We wound up drinking shots
in a tiny, empty joint
with a zinc bar and The Pogues,
for our benefit, on repeat.

I can still see the barman
smiling and pouring again –
glad of the company
and insisting in Hebrew that we stay.

Outside, the soldiers prowled:
walking backwards, as they do,
taking sweeping, hopeful aim
around the windows and the walls.

The same palaver earlier,
north of Bethlehem –
lending muscle to teenagers
wearing kippahs and high-slung Uzis

who escorted, if that's the word,
a rowdy parade of pilgrims –
pale insistent people we filmed
on their march to Rachel's Tomb.

Anyway, we talked about the syndrome
and who, should I lose my reason here,
I might become. Not the Messiah,
that's for sure, or either of the Johns,

and, if not some lesser-known apostle,
then some tired local nobody
who might remark to the passing Yeshua,
that while well impressed

by miracles and cures,
and by camels and by needles' eyes,
he was yet to be convinced, especially here,
by this constant turning of the cheek.

Jesus, was I ever more uneasy in a place?
And I'm not referring to the bar – not with Art
and The Pogues and a barman from Tiberias
who was, at the end of the day, the salt of the earth.

Breandrum

All the dapper men who used to say hello.
All the glamorous, lipsticked women
who'd ask how things were going

at university or at work.
All the shopkeepers, street-sweepers,
the dentist who pulled a broken tooth,

the nurse who stitched me up after a fall,
a man I watched in awe
as he wallpapered the hall,

stairs and landing. All the teachers,
plumbers, doctors, sparks; all the rakes
and chancers I'd chat with

on the Diamond – now planted in the clay.
What comes to mind, don't ask, is Dostoyevsky
buried in the rainy heart of Petrograd,

and those times I walked in line past Lenin,
Elvis, John XXIII and Mao Zedong –
just made my solemn way with no false moves.

The only one I ever skipped
was the tomb of Jesus Christ himself –
too many possibilities and always some dispute

about the true and definite space
(and where, it's said, He didn't lie for long
in any case). Yet more confusion to embrace.

But here, at home, I know the names on every definite stone –
parents of the boys at school and, hard to believe, my own.
I greet them from the path. My shadow is thrown.

A Wise Woman

She lives on a street that runs to the river;
the door open to sandstone flags just wide enough
for passers-by to tip along, sideways, on their way
to the shore. I sometimes think of pirates, cut-throats,
bandits with daggers, cutlasses and clubs.

Most days, she's stationed there, as broad
as she is long, arms folded, apron on,
eager for news of who is dead – or close to it –
and who is not. Mad for the rum tale, the rumour
and the chat. A sale in Tully's. A wedding. A crash.

The darkness in behind her smells of bread and buns –
everything snug, low-ceilinged, ancient, cool,
the hallway painted mustard and deep, blood red.
The Sacred Heart, the lamp, the crucifix, JFK and Jackie on a plate.
A cat that whispers, stretches, snores.

Our Lady of Perpetual Succour gleams Byzantine
and flat. The calendar – stuck on January – has Vincent Strambi
gazing at the wireless – on but inaudible and jammed at Athlone
for the Angelus and Mass. In the cupboard, the Camp Coffee
has been standing a lifetime – mysterious, unused.

This morning, in summer sun, I find her in the yard,
seated heavily on a painted stick-back chair. Her dress
goes with the geraniums; her sunglasses have yellow frames;
her hair is in a sea-shell bun. Whiter than the walls around her,
her feet are folding water in an old tin bath.

A wise woman, I greet and garland her with flowers –
stolen tokens taken from the Lough – mayflower
and the yellow irises that we call flags.
Her fingers drum the flowers of her dress –
the sunlit, bright material taut from knee to knee.

Between herself and myself, the mangle and the bath,
there's hardly room to move, so I sit before her on the ground
and deliver, with precision, all the news.
Everything is perfect, purposeful, infinite.
And then some questions of my own.

What is eternal? What is unchanging?
What is present in the human soul? What was it existed
before existence itself? And before non-existence, what?
Tapping the water gently with her toes, she answers me
methodically. Incredibly. Our own Upanishad.

Wintering Blackcap

It was the poet Clare mistook you for a nightingale
when, in March, he heard your far-too-early notes.
And Messiaen, a man I heard (or may have heard) in Paris
christened you St. Francis when he listened
high above Assisi – that rocky hermitage at Carceri
where the saint once prayed and joshed with birds.

Could it be that, in our turn, you mistake me for a poet –
out writing on his hat and pacing the crumping snow?
Or composer – imagine that – noting down the convolutions
of your song. Perhaps some poor Franciscan in his tiny prison,
or a German farmer, abroad in a bony orchard,
cursing quietly the new bad weather on the way?

But, for now, until things change, you're dependable still –
King Harry, Coal Hoodie, Mock Nightingale.
You have been my friend this long uneasy winter.
There, without fail, to feast on bits of food I've offered up –
balls of fat, softening apples roughly halved.
Of course I half-ignore you; you half-ignore me back.

Walking the Dog

Rosco pays the poet's full attention –
alert to every track and trace,
and all those tiny airborne sounds
that constitute the perfect silences –
birdsong, airplanes, mowers;
that tinny, rhythmic hammering
from half a mile away.

He misses nothing.
And if and when I drift, he stops
to bring me back; his stubborn tug
like a pike at the Pump House Shore
just as rod and line and trailing bait –
even the creaking boat itself –
have been, in reverie, forgotten.

I love our danders round the block.
A dreamtime circuit, a pavement loop
where all is memory and wonder.
Yesterday, this warm, black, biodegradable bag
of what my mother called dog's dirt
had me thinking – *Jack steps home
from market with his bag of magic beans.*

This morning it's a heavy, leather purse
tossed by a dandy to an urchin in the street;
when I hep it in my hand it rings aloud
with gleaming sovereigns. Rosco sits
and tilts his head, and together we ponder
what is possible – what is magical –
in this unexpected fortune of jingle and tap.

The Local Heron

The local heron passes
low above the house.
He's made of canvas,
wood and string –
wide and wonky, sailing
through his own
half-hearted utterance –
Leonardo's flying machine,
just about airborne.

If he goes any slower
he'll tumble and crash
like a broken umbrella.
His brief metallic echo
is the hacked-up feather
of a poem
sucked ruinously away.
He doesn't seem to care.
He doesn't know I'm here

to always overplay the thing –
the cloud-grey camouflage,
the mechanism of his wings.
He could be my overcast brother,
or just another drunken hunter
heading home,
too familiar with the route.
Later, in the redwood tree,
he'll wade the darkening canopy.

Mweenish

Two blue sharks entered the shallows
and swerved – black shadows – between you
and the shore. To implore you to swim was useless.
Where would you go? The horizon was far.

Sun-blinded, I stumbled seawards
and there, with my botanist's tweezers,
I lifted both by their dorsal fins
and dropped them in a jar.

Meanwhile, you just kicked and splashed,
unaware that time and fate and even scale
had shifted once again. I walked backwards to the *machair*,
my captives glaring in a swirl of sun.

That night I put them on the windowsill
beside the harebells, the hibiscus and the bedstraw
and fed them tiny bits of chicken, mince and flies.
In the morning just the one, twice the size, was left.

In silhouette, he stared at me all day, circling clockwise
and sometimes, in a rage, making such whirlpools
as might overturn the jar – outpour himself, full shark again,
on the slate of the kitchen floor.

At midnight, on the far side of the island,
I slipped him to the waves of another sea entirely.
I took pictures in the darkness, but none came out.
And now, my beautiful child, you will never believe me.

Kerrymount Avenue

Beckett's bookmark
was a holy picture –

St. Francis Preaching to the Birds –
slipped in certain places

throughout his precious Dante
for sixty-something years.

The artist is Giotto.
When asked by the Pope

to demonstrate his skill,
he drew, by hand, the perfect circle.

So I wonder was it him
the playwright so admired?

The artist as opposed to Francis?
Or was it, regardless of either,

the image itself that,
thanks to both, existed?

Or maybe it was just the birds –
among them blackbirds, bitterns,

magpies, finches, geese
and a couple of Rockabill choughs.

And then, of course, the notion itself –
the very idea – that they wouldn't budge

until they'd heard the friar preach
and he, laughing, had blessed them one by one.

The Easel

The easel is all seized up. It stands like a human frame
copied, with a young man's enthusiasm,

from a book called *How to Draw and Paint*.
The pelvis is crooked, the shoulders tilt and feint.

It's here behind me in the shed – an easel my father made
by hand. And these bits of faded paint are the cadmium red

of my mother's skirt, the cerulean blue of my mother's blouse.
He looks away, then back again and she, the perfect sitter,
    holds his gaze.

Bottles

A small boy enters the enclosure –
an iron, floodlit maze of bottle-banks.
It's very late, and he should not be here.
His hunched-up father watches from the car.

The boy works quickly, relentlessly,
shoving bottle after bottle after bottle
into a dark and open O – each one
exploding brutally like a brawl

in a stinking hull, or in the belly
of a bomb-proof bunker in the sand.
The glass is always green or brown or clear;
the bottles mostly vodka, brandy, wine.

When the job is done, he backs away.
He keeps the bags for again.
His father, straightening, starts the car
The boy has fed the Minotaur.

Nocturne II

I know when the fox is close –
the alarms of insomniac blackbirds
nesting foolishly under lights,
their heads turned by endless day.

Magpies too – all ratchety – and then
the yapping envy of domesticated dogs
tormented at windows and flaps – the old foxy stink
mocking what little they have left.

It's warm tonight, and not a breath. The universe
has me spotted, noted and forgotten about by now –
here in a busted armchair waiting for whatever comes:
vixen, hedgehog, leopard, ghost.

Grief, I tell myself, is never sadness unaccompanied.
In the apple tree I see an apple slowly turn,
unscrew itself and fall. It hits the ground
and lies there stunned – wondering what to do.

The Shed

A coffee cup – ceramic and Greek –
is balanced on the saddle of a bike.

I can hardly move these days for bikes,
piled on each other like anonymous bones

in the Catacombs of Paris or Rome.
Ancient memories now of barrow, tumulus

and souterrain – my shambles of a hideout,
my through-other dog-house, my ruined lair.

This is my shanty, my bothy, my Batcave,
my dacha and my swineherd's hut –

ramshackle meeting-house for aislings
and spiders, angels, demons and shades.

Here, of an evening, I have both flown
and fallen, sailed the seas and sunk.

To think that beneath this wasted mirror ball
a silent hedgehog killed a rattlesnake,

that swans once landed in a snowstorm –
went flying on a frozen lake.

Ravens

I was awakened by ravens –
the eyes and ears of Odin,
unwelcome in my walled-in garden.

Had I been taken in my sleep?
Lifted, bed and all, and abandoned
on an icy Nordic crag?

Was I seasick and somehow on the Ark?
Were these the battlements of the local Church
of Ireland, or the city of Uruk?

I asked them outright what they wanted,
these ravens, their old Maamturk croak
so wrong for a garden in Dublin

yet right for a morning in Midgard
and dreams full of dying and ghosts
and glimpses of Gilgamesh.

What news would they bring back to Odin?
That a man, confused, had followed them
to a juniper tree and, in blue daylight,

had welcomed them with human speech;
hailed them as protectors, and shared with them
his meal of sweetened oats and toasted bread.

The Roof Space

Not an attic with a skylight
and sheeted, antique furniture,
not an attic with a rocking horse,
a hat-stand and trunks full of clothes
you might use for fancy dress,

it was instead a treacherous place –
unlit, unfloored and unexplored.
Put a foot wrong in the roof space
and you'd fall through the ceiling
of the room below.

The entrance was a plywood square –
framed and high above your head;
an unsteady slab when you'd push it up,
then slide it sideways to the left.
No ladder either,

so I was always amazed
when my father would haul himself up
like a gymnast and, torch in hand,
wade lightly over clouds of insulation.
Maybe seeing to the tank or fixing a cable.

My old pram was lying sideways
across the joists; and a cardboard box
of photographs no one ever got around to.
Then, job done, he'd return to us,
dropping in a long, unhurried hang.

There was a starling trapped there once.
Loud at first, it panicked in the dark
but then was quiet as an anchorite.
The last thing it expected was a rumble in the earth;
a square of sunshine in the opening sky below.

Never Show Me Where The Falcons Are

Never show me where the falcons are.
Don't take me to the towers and point them out.
I'll only steal your observations, your perfect notes
and sketches, and slide them slyly into poems.

I'd have your life if you let me – a well-lived life
as lived by you but, these days, unavailable to me
when all I seem to do is hover in the darkest space
between the bed and the ceiling – more *volière*

than estuary, beach or open bog.
So don't invite me. Be careful around me.
Guard, with your life, your well-earned glossary
of sacred words like *tiercel, mantle* and *pitch*.

In any event, I'd only embarrass the birds –
coming at it, as I do, from a half-tame garden
with little winter sun. And so I must refuse your news
of a peregrine's perfect stoop, or be forever in the wrong.

Waxwings

There was a time when men believed
that, in the thickest forests of our fairy tales,
waxwings glowed like candles in the dark.
Birds in cages used as torches in the mediaeval night.

So if you wonder why I'm standing at the window
watching waxwings in the fading light,
I'm waiting like the cobbler for the flicker –
a luminescence that will prove the notion right.